THIS BOOK BELONGS TO

MIRACLES of JESUS

Written and Illustrated by
BROOKE MALIA MANN

DESERET BOOK

Salt Lake City, Utah

To my biggest fan, Randall,

who keeps cheering me on in every way.

© 2019 Brooke Malia Mann

All rights reserved. No part of this book may be reproduced in any form or by any means without permission in writing from the publisher, Deseret Book Company, at permissions@deseretbook.com or PO Box 30178, Salt Lake City, Utah 84130. This work is not an official publication of The Church of Jesus Christ of Latter-day Saints. The views expressed herein are the responsibility of the author and do not necessarily represent the position of the Church or of Deseret Book Company.

DESERET BOOK is a registered trademark of Deseret Book Company.

Visit us at DeseretBook.com

Library of Congress Cataloging-in-Publication Data
Names: Mann, Brooke Malia, author, illustrator.
Title: Miracles of Jesus / Brooke Malia Mann.
Description: Salt Lake City, Utah : Deseret Book, [2019]. | Includes bibliographical references.
Identifiers: LCCN 2018039961 | ISBN 9781629725222 (hardbound : alk. paper)
Subjects: LCSH: Jesus Christ—Miracles—Juvenile literature. | LCGFT: Picture books.
Classification: LCC BT366.3 .M27 2019 | DDC 232.9/55—dc23
LC record available at https://lccn.loc.gov/2018039961

Printed in China   10/2018
RR Donnelley, Shenzhen, China

10 9 8 7 6 5 4 3 2 1

This is the true story of our **SAVIOR, JESUS CHRIST**, the Son of God. He was part mortal and part God, and He performed **MANY MIRACLES** while He walked the Earth and even after He died.

When
JESUS was
BORN, . . .

As a **YOUNG BOY** of only twelve, Jesus taught adults at the temple in Jerusalem.

When He was
BAPTIZED
by John . . .

... the **HOLY GHOST** appeared as a dove and the Father spoke from heaven.

Jesus HELPED HIS MOTHER and the other guests at a wedding by turning WATER INTO WINE.

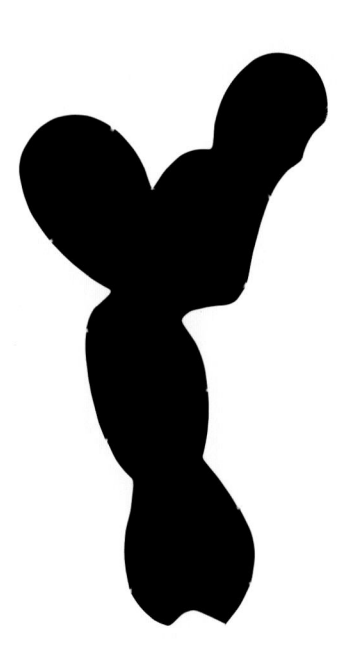

With
only five
loaves of
BREAD
and two
FISHES, . . .

...JESUS FED 5,000 people.

On the top of a MOUNTAIN, . . .

. . . Jesus Christ SPOKE WITH the ancient PROPHETS Moses and Elijah.

He **HEALED** people
who were born **BLIND**, and
people who were
DEAF or **LAME**.

Jesus also
HEALED LEPERS
and many other **SICK** people.

He LOVED LITTLE CHILDREN . . .

During His last meal, Christ fed His friends
BREAD AND WINE as the first **SACRAMENT**.

This created a powerful symbol to help us **REMEMBER HIM.**

In the Garden of Gethsemane,
JESUS TOOK UPON HIMSELF
the sins, pains, and heartaches
of every person who has lived
or who will ever live.

Then, when He **DIED ON THE CROSS**
of Calvary, the skies darkened
and the ground quaked.

He was **RESURRECTED** three days later.

As the resurrected Lord, Jesus **VISITED HIS FRIENDS** and filled their nets to the brim with fish.

Although we can't see Him now,

JESUS CHRIST

is still **PERFORMING MIRACLES.**

And one day, one of the **GREATEST MIRACLES** of all will happen.

Scripture References

BLESSED ART THOU
Matthew 16:16; John 4:14; Galatians 4:4.

PEACE BE STILL
Matthew 8:23–27; Mark 4:36–41; Luke 8:22–25.

OF SUCH IS THE KINGDOM OF GOD
Mark 10:13–16; Luke 18:15–17.

BLESSED ART THOU
Luke 1:26–35.

ARISE
Matthew 9:18–19, 23–26; Mark 5:22–24, 35–42; Luke 8:41–42, 49–56.

IN REMEMBRANCE OF ME
Matthew 26:26–28; Mark 14:22–24; Luke 22:19–20.

GLORY TO GOD
Luke 2:11–14; see also Matthew 2:9–10.

THEY DID ALL EAT
Matthew 14:15–21; Mark 6:37–44; Luke 9:13–17; John 6:5–14.

TARRY YE HERE
Matthew 26:36–44; Mark 14: 32–39; Luke 22:39–44; see also Isaiah 53:4–5; Romans 6:23; 2 Corinthians 5:19; Hebrews 2:17; 1 John 1:7; 4:10.

THE CHILD JESUS
Luke 2:41–50.

BE OF GOOD CHEER
Matthew 14:24–27; Mark 6:47–51; John 6:17–21.

DARKNESS OVER
Matthew 27:45, 50–51; Mark 15:33, 37–38; Luke 23:44–45.

BORN OF WATER
Matthew 3:13–17; see also Mark 1:9–11; Luke 3:21–22.

THEY SAW HIS GLORY
Matthew 17:1–3; Mark 9:2–4; Luke 9:28–32.

WHOM SEEKEST THOU?
Matthew 28:1–8; Mark 16:1–11; Luke 24:1–12; John 20:11–18.

THE BEGINNING OF MIRACLES
John 2:1–11.

I WAS BLIND, NOW I SEE
John 9:1–7; see also Matthew 9:27–30; 15:30; Mark 7:32–37; 8:22–25; 10:49–52; Luke 18:41–43.

CAST THE NET AND YE SHALL FIND
John 21:3–6.

POWER TO FORGIVE SINS
Matthew 9:2–7; Mark 2:1–12; Luke 5:18–25; see also Luke 7:46–50.

GIVING HIM THANKS
Luke 17:11–19; see also Matthew 4:23–24; 9:35; Mark 1:40–42; 6:56; Luke 4:40; 5:12–15.

BELIEVE IN HIM
John 5:28–29; 14:18–21; Acts 1:11; 5:12; 24:15; 1 Corinthians 12:7–10; 15:21–22.